MW01007191

# CATHOLIC ANSWERS TO QUESTIONS ABOUT THE NEW AGE MOVEMENT

Ronald Quillo
Foreword by Philip St. Romain

**LIGUORI**
PUBLICATIONS
One Liguori Drive
Liguori, MO 63057-9999
(314) 464-2500

Imprimi Potest:
James Shea, C.SS.R.
Provincial, St. Louis Province
The Redemptorists

Imprimatur:
+ Paul Zipfel, V.G.
Auxiliary Bishop, Archdiocese of St. Louis

ISBN 0-89243-764-2
Library of Congress Catalog Card Number: 94-79998

Copyright © 1995, Ronald Quillo
Printed in the United States of America
First Edition

Cover design by Wendy Barnes

For those
I am pleased to call
My children
> Nathan,
> Heather,
> Anne,
> Jason,
> Jeremy,
> Amy,
> Gabriel

Each of whom
In a special way
Has brought
A new age
Into my life

# Contents

# Foreword

Very few times in the history of Christianity has the Church encountered systems of thought which significantly challenged and renewed her way of seeing things. One of these was the discovery of Greek philosophy, which influenced Saint Augustine and ultimately led to the theological synthesis of Saint Thomas Aquinas. Until the Second Vatican Council, Saint Thomas' theology was considered foundational for all ministers. It is still a helpful tool in the right hands.

Another great encounter began with the Enlightenment of the eighteenth century and continues to this day as we grapple with the implications of modern physics, technology, and psychology. Saint Thomas' theology can help us with some of this, but frequently there are questions and issues about which he knew nothing. What would he have thought about evolution and original sin, or about genetic engineering? The biological assumptions that formed his thinking are no longer shared by most of today's theologians. We must stretch as we attempt to connect the new with the old. The Second Vatican Council was such an effort and represents the Church's response to the Enlightenment.

Another great encounter has barely begun. It is the meeting between Christianity and Eastern forms of religion and spirituality. The fathers of Vatican II wrote a friendly acknowledgment of this beginning and tried to set a few ground rules for its continuance. Little did they know, however, that within thirty years, many Catholic retreat houses would be offering retreats on Zen, Yoga, the enneagram, and tai chi chuan.

The New Age movement is an attempt to process these spiritual waves that are crashing about us. Drawing from the modern sciences, ancient philosophy, Christianity, Eastern religions, and nature religions, people in the New Age movement are attempting to forge a new understanding of the human condition and the means by which we are liberated. This understanding is derived not from philosophical reflection, but from experimentation and experience. New Age followers don't just want to understand spirituality, they want to know it firsthand.

What are Catholics to think about these encounters and the New Age movement? At one extreme are the archconservatives who feel very threatened by all of this. These are the people who labeled Saint Thomas Aquinas a heretic during his time and continue to do the same to Thomas Merton, Teilhard de Chardin, and Bede Griffiths. They see the New Age as a conspiracy responsible for almost all that (to them) is wrong with the Church today. Some of their books and television programs against the New Age are very popular with many Catholics, who by and large would like the Enlightenment and the encounter with the East to just go away. They won't go away, however, so the reactionary response will not prevail.

At the opposite extreme are the liberals who seem to compromise Catholic beliefs in their attempt to accommodate Catholicism to modern science and Eastern religions. These distortions range from believing in reincarnation to practicing witchcraft, consorting with the spirits of the dead, and accepting a guru as the incarnation of God. This is not true ecumenism, and it too will not prevail.

*Catholic Answers to Questions About the New Age Movement* avoids those two extremes. Ronald Quillo recognizes that there is much good in the New Age movement and much that is hazardous to one's faith. Refreshingly absent from this booklet are the diatribes of the reactionaries and the gushing enthusiasm of the liberals. Instead, we are given a sober and straightforward presentation of the many New Age practices from the viewpoint of an educated post-Vatican II Catholic. There is a great need for books like this.

PHILIP ST. ROMAIN
WICHITA, KANSAS

# INTRODUCTION

# On Newness and Novelty

The centuries-old, soon millennia-old, Roman Catholic Church has seen many things come and go—and sometimes return. Its heritage, shaped by experience, time, and inspiration, has helped create an institution rich in wisdom and blessings. This Church might therefore claim that there is nothing new under the sun. Such a pronouncement, though reflecting a profound sense of history, would indicate a narrowness not typically Catholic. It would also suggest an unwillingness to recognize the potential of what appears to be new but is actually something ages old presented in novel form. Yet Catholicism's many rites, theologies, customs, and institutions provide ample evidence that the Church has always been receptive to both newness and novelty. The characteristic diversity within Catholicism, where catholicity means universality, has not undermined the unity the Church has preserved by adopting only what suits its nature and mission.

In recent years the New Age movement has grown in popularity throughout the world. The current shape of the movement is primarily due to religious and secular currents of the nineteenth and twentieth centuries. Yet many New Age elements have even deeper roots that relate to beliefs and practices modern scholars tell us go back thousands of years. The attractiveness of these ancient visions and methodologies is partially explained by the compelling and novel way in which they are now presented and enjoyed. Though essentially a Western phenomenon, the New Age movement includes many features typical of Eastern cultures and religious traditions. The foreign and the new, like the proverbial greener grass on the other side, can appear through its novelty to offer more than we can readily find in our own backyards.

We can reject the new and the novel, claiming that innovation is disturbing and possibly disastrous. Or we can look kindly upon it, seeking what is valuable and useful. Recognizing historical developments when the Church's caution often resulted in excessive mistrust and division, the Second Vatican Council challenged Catholics and others to reach out in dialogue, to discern what common beliefs they share, and to work cooperatively as agents of improvement for our world. Christians believe that God must ultimately inspire this kind of change; human initiative is but a partner in the process. Christians also maintain that humans must adhere only to beliefs and practices that serve divine designs.

This booklet about the New Age movement is written in a spirit of dialogue. Many Catholics today are curious yet wary of the movement. They appreciate help in understanding its principle features and knowing how these stand in light of Catholic teachings. Catholics want to know what is beneficial in this New Age, which often appears with fascinating novelty. They have probably heard much that is negative, that judges the movement as pernicious and a threat to Christianity. They, therefore, want to know what is valid and what is unacceptable. But they deserve a presentation and analysis based on the guidelines originally set by Vatican II and now maintained by the Pontifical Council for Inter-religious Dialogue in Rome. The following discussion, though neither exhaustive nor the final word, intends to provide such assistance to Catholics and other interested persons.

# ONE

# *A Cult or What?*

*What is the New Age movement?*

During the last few decades, especially since the late 1960s, individuals and groups throughout the Western world have discovered a common interest in the spiritual realm. Convinced that preoccupation with the purely material and merely physical inhibits happiness and personal growth, they have set their sights beyond everyday experience, hoping to find new joy and better means of improving their own lives and the lives of others. Together they look beyond the everyday, seeking to become part of a process in which human experiences are renewed and all of earth's life is nurtured. They believe that all things function best—and the greatest capacities of all things are realized—when everyone and everything evidence the wholesome and healing influence of what is eminently spiritual. An individual must work toward a greater wholeness where body, mind, and spirit are brought into new harmony. Societies must strive for reconciliation and peace among all people and work for a new relationship between humanity and the earth's ecology so that both truly benefit.

Individuals and groups who view reality this way do not generally fit into established and commonly accepted categories. These persons sometimes profess "unusual" philosophies that appear foreign by prevailing Western standards. They may participate in "strange" practices not usually associated with common Western customs. Because these persons are introducing something novel or new, often claiming that the ways of the present age are radically changing, they have come to be called members of the "New Age movement." But the designation *New Age* is very flexible; naming specific boundaries of the movement is quite problematic. Hundreds, even thousands, of philosophies, perspectives, theories, practices, and techniques belong in the category of beliefs and lifestyles considered unusual or countercultural. Also problematic is whether the interests of this New Age constitute a *movement*. Certain shifts are observed. But without a strong centralizing or organizing pattern, these tendencies can be called a "movement" only in a broad sense. *New Age* has thus emerged as a convenient description of anyone or anything that is either vaguely or clearly associated with this novel vision, with this characteristic interest in spirituality and harmony.

A vision of reality primarily concerned with harmonious relationships is sometimes called holistic. Established Western religions, including Christianity, are interested in the realm of the spiritual, an essential element of the biblical teaching regarding the kingdom of God. And Christianity understands that this kingdom, involving salvation for humanity and all creation, is characterized by the harmonious relationships among all creatures and between all creation and God. The New Age movement does not turn primarily to Christianity, however, for its vision and practices. The holistic outlook of the New Age movement and the variety of techniques through which New Age enthusiasts seek personal, social, and environmental transformation have a number of sources. These include Eastern non-Christian religions, Native American religions, philosophy, modern psychology, holistic health, the new physics, ecology, and the domain of the paranormal or extrasensory perception (ESP). Although it is possible to identify some general features that are typical of the New Age movement, it is difficult and often impossible to name distinguishing characteristics that mark each and every person associated with the movement.

### But aren't occultists, entertainers, and media personalities the main representatives of the New Age?

These persons surely receive the most publicity, but they are minor elements of the New Age movement. Some media personalities have captured something of the authentic spirit of the New Age and have attracted a following. When these celebrities expose their fans to helpful influences, helping others find refreshing and healing paths in their lives, these public persons enhance the credibility of the New Age movement. Shirley

MacLaine, a reputable example, has influenced many though she is neither a scholar nor a professed religious leader. MacLaine and others like her, however, are sometimes misunderstood because of misrepresentation or because of a focus on the most sensational or unconventional elements of their work.

On the other hand, there are a few persons—very few—with malicious intents who are identified with the New Age either by mistake or because of their own wrongful claims. They may use some things associated with the New Age, but this does not make them typical of the New Age movement. Evil-minded persons have also "borrowed" some Christian practices and elements of worship, attempting to associate themselves with Christianity. Their practices, however, have only distorted Christianity. We must be aware that some who claim to be part of the movement do not share the New Age's humanitarian and benevolent interests. We should not associate the New Age with Satanism or occult groups that are manipulative, ungodly, or evil. The *Catechism of the Catholic Church* speaks of these superstitious or malicious groups when it warns of the irreligiousness found in "attempts to tame occult powers, so as to place them at one's service and have a supernatural power over others" (2117).

The overwhelming majority of New Age followers are benevolent, primarily interested in or dedicated to improving themselves, others, and the world. Some of them attempt to utilize psychic or paranormal influences often associated with the occult, but their reliance on these influences is not malicious and does not make them a cult. The New Age movement is not an exclusive group and does not try to brainwash and separate persons from everyday life and relationships. The movement is considerate, respectful, and anxious to work with society to make the world a better place.

### Do those in the New Age movement consider themselves a privileged group?

Generally they are tolerant and accepting. Acknowledging that individuals, groups, and societies have developed many methods for attaining peace and happiness, proponents of the New Age respect variety in both the secular and religious domains. They cooperate with all established philosophies, ideologies, and religions. However, the New Age movement is not exempt from the human tendency toward elitism, thinking that *my* or *our* way is the best. Occasionally some within the movement will criticize insincerity, hollowness, superficiality, and other perceived faults, implying that these flaws are typical of a particular group like an organized religion. But these are minority opinions among those associated with the New Age.

### Is the New Age interest in the spiritual a way of relating to God as understood by believing Christians?

The Bible clearly presents Jewish and Christian faiths as unique and special ways through which God is authentically known. With less intensity but with notable regularity, the Bible also clearly reveals how God as both creator and redeemer cares for all humanity and desires the salvation of all. Paul teaches that even without a biblical sense of faith, persons can still know God and are answerable to divinely ordained standards of conduct (Romans 1:20; 2:15). The Second Vatican Council, while professing that "the fullness of...religious life" is found in Christ, reminded us that the various religions of the world approach the divine mystery in different ways and can teach us much about religious values. Furthermore, the Council encouraged Christians to enter into respectful dialogue and collaborate with others to promote "the spiritual and moral truths" that are part of their lives and cultures. The Council specifically mentioned Hinduism and Buddhism, Eastern religions whose teachings are particularly valued in the New Age movement. These religions are devoutly directed toward the truth of God (*Declaration on the Relation of the Church to Non-Christian Religions*, 2). Therefore, the *Catechism of the Catholic Church* says that these persons, though they do not know Christ, "can be saved" if they seek truth and do God's will as they understand it (1260).

Moreover, proponents and devotees of the New Age typically associate their interests with biblical themes and the goals of all religions. New Age proponents even relate their work to that of eminent Christian scholars such as the Catholic theologian and anthropologist Father Pierre Teilhard de Chardin. There are good reasons, therefore, for acknowledging that the New Age, with its characteristic reverence for divinity, shares much with those who believe in the God of Jesus Christ.

## Why is consciousness so important in the New Age movement?

The New Age is interested in personal transformation so that individuals can have a new awareness of themselves and their particular responsibilities. This heightened self-identity and higher consciousness is closely linked to a more sensitive conscience and greater conscientiousness. The emphasis is not simply on intellectual awareness or intelligence, though one of the New Age's historical roots is a religious movement known as New Thought. Today some refer to the New Age as the New Consciousness or as the Consciousness movement. The knowledge that characterizes this awareness is both cognitive and moral, involving both new mental awareness and a new ethical sense; with this consciousness persons are inclined to care for others and assume a proper and beneficial role in society. This knowledge, arising from the mind as well as the heart, influences both understanding and behavior—a very practical and helpful knowledge. The Bible typically equates this kind of awareness with wisdom, understanding, knowledge, and similar qualities. The prophet Isaiah names some of these aptitudes (11:2) and Catholic tradition calls them gifts of the Holy Spirit. These forms of awareness bring great spiritual peace and joy while also inclining believers toward admirable moral conduct.

## Why is the New Age movement so frequently condemned or criticized?

There are many reasons. Some critics simply have an intense enthusiasm for their own views. Others misunderstand what the New Age really is, drawing their conclusions from false information regarding the New Age or focusing solely on the activities of persons who do not fittingly represent New Age ways. Other critics are preoccupied with what every group or movement has: faults and failings. Sadly, we must admit that fault-finding comes easily for most of us. We do this as individuals and as members of social groups, races, and religions. Throughout history—even today—we observe how certain groups have become objects of scorn, ridicule, and persecution. Jews, African-Americans, Catholics, and others have suffered abuse.

Psychologists tell us we frequently ridicule or persecute others because we see in them, sometimes incorrectly, the very weaknesses that we ourselves possess. Jesus also observes this human tendency: "With the judgment you make you will be judged" (Matthew 7:2). He means, among other things, that often the negative qualities we see in others—anger or injustice, for example—are really weaknesses or sins we bear within us, though we may be unaware of these faults. This kind of critical attitude may account for some of the negative judgments others make about the New Age. Still other critics have carefully examined the movement according to their own beliefs and concluded that the New Age movement is threatening, dangerous, and evil. Catholics seeking to familiarize themselves with the New Age can reserve judgment, remain open, be willing to dialogue respectfully, and reason to their conclusions in light of a personal faith that is suitably nurtured and guided by Scripture and the Church's traditions.

### Can Christians be led away from the faith by becoming involved in New Age practices?

It depends on *how* Christians become involved. They can embrace the New Age in a way that contradicts Church beliefs. When Christians find a new spiritual home amid beliefs not explicitly Christian, they leave the institutional church. This represents a different way of living; the church considers this a loss. The Vatican's *General Catechetical Directory* observes that Christian experiments with divination, a common New Age practice, has induced "in some places a lapse into syncretism" (7), an improper incorporation of non-Christian elements into Christian life. The *Catechism of the Catholic Church* further cautions that superstition, attaching more spiritual significance to something than it actually has, violates true religious practice (2110-2111).

Christians can, however, find certain elements of the New Age attractive—prayers or meditation, perhaps—and use them profitably without diminishing essential Christian beliefs and practices. Some New Age techniques, whether borrowed from Eastern religions or other spiritual traditions like the Native American, are compatible with Christian dispositions and virtues. Yoga postures (breathing and relaxation that assist spiritual awareness) and sweat lodges (heat and tranquility that cleanse the body and soul) can help believers grow in a distinctly Christian faith. Other techniques, including visualization and guided imagery (the imagination purposely used to heighten spiritual awareness), have precedents in Christian tradition. Saint Ignatius of Loyola suggested various methods of visualizing scenes from Scripture and using biblically-inspired imagery. New Age prayer and meditation is not really new.

The Vatican's Congregation for the Doctrine of the Faith, with the approval of Pope John Paul II, has published a *Letter to the Bishops of the Catholic Church on Some Aspects of Christian Meditation*. Giving particular attention to Hinduism and Buddhism, the Congregation clearly states that merely identifying a practice as non-Christian does not mean it must be excluded from Christian interest and usage. Noting the pope had preached that "any method of prayer is valid insofar as it is inspired by Christ and leads to Christ," the letter carefully observes that practices like Eastern meditation and other prayer forms can be utilized by Christians as long as the use does not lead to a loss of personal faith that is manifestly Christian. A believer in Christ enjoys, through the power of the Holy Spirit, a personal relationship with the Father. This relationship can be disturbed if non-Christian methodology becomes a substitute for—rather than an aid to—prayer that is part of authentic Christian faith supported by divine grace (2,3,12,16,20,23).

### Why, then, should we bother with New Age practices?

There are times when a new element introduced into our religious practice can help revitalize our faith and bring new perspectives to it. The Christmas tree illustrates how Christianity has historically incorporated pagan symbols into its customs and devotions. The decorated tree helps us experience Christ's light in our homes. Similarly, a New Age practice or technique like meditation can often help us recapture a true Christian spirit of prayer. Variety adds spice even to religious life. Turning to the New Age for such diversity should, of course, involve a trust that what is good will rightfully serve our beliefs. Novelty in this case cannot be an end in itself. We disservice our faith when we crave only novelty; we do this when we experiment frivolously even with elements well-established in Christian tradition, for example, using holy water superstitiously rather than reverently. In the letter mentioned above, the Vatican Congregation for the Doctrine of the Faith points out that even an established Christian method of prayer can, if not properly directed toward God, become an obstacle to spiritual growth (27).

### But isn't relying on a technique the same as trying to accomplish good without God's grace?

It can be, if our reliance is unaccompanied by faith. This applies to established Christian techniques too. True religious growth, and the kind of inner peace that comes through the presence of the Holy Spirit, is achieved only because the grace of God, a gift freely given, assists us. The Catholic Church and other Christian churches teach this clearly. Most spiritual masters, whether Christian or not, also teach that no technique by itself produces a desired religious goal. That goal can be attained only as a gift from God and as a sign of divine presence. Specific techniques and devotions merely prepare us, disposing us to receive divine blessing. So whether we recite a mantra, pray the rosary, or rely on techniques from other sources, we draw closer to God only because, in opening ourselves to God through faith, God gives us the privilege and power of this rewarding intimacy.

# TWO

~~~~~~~~~~~~~~~~~~~~~~~~~~~~

# *Prayer and Super Power*

### *What is a mantra?*

In some Eastern religions, Hinduism and Buddhism for example, worshipers use a word or phrase when meditating or praying; this helps them focus, remain centered, stay in touch with the holy, and attain higher states of spiritual consciousness. By slowly and repeatedly speaking, whispering, or thinking the word or phrase, a mantra, they avoid distractions and become more relaxed; this helps them more easily realize a higher spiritual state and greater intimacy with the Divine. The rhythmic repetition soothes the spirit and the steady utterance serves the sense of dedication, the sincere desire to advance spiritually. Many New Age proponents have borrowed this technique to achieve higher consciousness and a sense of spiritual renewal.

In Eastern Christianity the Jesus Prayer, a short act of praise and contrition, has been used for centuries. Proponents claim it helps them achieve the highest states of religious ecstasy. The rosary can also serve as a mantra. The rhythmic and devotional repetition of the Hail Mary is worshipful persistence in a steadfast faith that inclines believers to rely on Christ, the Father, and the Holy Spirit through the intercession of Mary, the mother of Jesus and the Church. The rosary goes beyond ordinary mantras, however, because it involves purposeful meditation on various scenes associated with each decade or set of ten Hail Marys. As a special Christian prayer, the rosary thus combines advantages of both the mantra and guided imagery.

### *Is there something spiritual about New Age music?*

The musical category, *New Age*, has become so broad that we find it difficult to specify exactly what kinds of music belong here. Marketing and production decisions, rather than the distinctive qualities of the music itself, frequently specify a composition or performance for this category. The music therefore resembles the movement that we designate *New Age*; determining what belongs and what does not is often problematic.

Nevertheless, like the movement, New Age music possesses some very general features we can call typical. Its nontraditional sound does not clearly fit into established categories—classical, folk, jazz, blues, or popular—although we might loosely identify the performers by style: jazz or classical, for instance. The uncommon character of New Age music gives it an ethereal or "spacey" sound, an idiosyncrasy characterized by lack of a distinct melody. The tune seems to go nowhere, flowing without direction and making no abrupt alterations in pitch, tempo, and volume. The calming nature of much New Age music recalls one of its original purposes: to induce relaxation and facilitate meditation. The occasional inclusion of natural sounds like bird calls and ocean waves heightens spiritual interests: joy in the beauty of creation or reflection on environmental concerns.

Like most religions of the world, Christianity has recognized music's power to enhance the spiritual value of prayer, worship, and communal celebration. Catholic sensitivity for sacramentality, God's loving presence in the tangible, utilizes numerous forms of sacred music. Some, folk music for example, closely resemble familiar established secular styles, while others are distinctly "churchy" or otherworldly in tone. Gregorian chant is one example. In liturgical settings the free flow of some instrumental interludes, especially when improvised, conveys an air resembling the New Age idiom. Catholics are free to determine to what extent they find New Age music aesthetically and spiritually uplifting.

**Do New Age devotees, no matter what they are doing to advance spiritually, disregard the need for grace because they think they have divine powers?**

Generally, their teachings do not speak of grace but reflect a great deal of confidence in the human capacity to step beyond egoism or selfishness into a state of higher consciousness. New Age views of reality, including human nature, are often pantheistic. These perspectives, borrowed in part from Hinduism and Buddhism, view God or the divine essence as the true identity of all things: everything is regarded as God, all things and all persons. This sounds strange to our Western and Christian ears. Because of environment and education, we take for granted the individuality of everything: a *thing* is that *thing* and nothing more; an *individual* is that *individual* and nothing more. Our faith leads us to accept that all reality, and therefore all persons, are creations of God and therefore are distinct from the divine essence. Furthermore, we believe this distinction has been negatively intensified by sin. As Christians, we profess our need for divine help and grace so that we can be saved from the effects of separation from God and advance in happiness and virtue. We can rely on God's grace with great confidence.

In the pantheistic view, advancement in happiness and virtue—both of which are part of higher consciousness—means people must become increasingly clear about their own divinity and the divinity of everything else. The more they appreciate this specialness that identifies all reality, the more they appreciate themselves, others, and the world; they are less inclined to treat themselves, others, and the world unbecomingly. From this perspective, looking another person in the eye is really God looking at God's own self. Pantheism, therefore, gives a peculiar turn to the rule "Love your neighbor as yourself" (Matthew 22:39). Christians believe this means "love your neighbor to the same degree and in the same way that you love yourself." Through God's grace, this love is part of the joyful and reconciling love in the kingdom of God on earth and in heaven. The pantheistic interpretation of the same rule is "love your neighbor; when you do so, you are really loving yourself." Enlivened by his Christian perspective, Paul views love and service to others as a form of self-love in a broad sense insofar as all Christians are one, members of the Body of Christ, the community of faith and fellowship (1 Corinthians 12:27–13:13).

Such love is possible, New Age proponents say, because it is the activation of their true divine nature. Grace, therefore, needs no mention. The appearance of differences—whether of individual persons or things from one another, or of all these realities from God—is, according to this view, a great illusion. The more people open their eyes to the divine beauty of all things, the more they will love one another, the more they will take care their world, and the happier they will be. All persons possess these powers, the New Age says; people *are* such powers and need to learn to rely on them.

Not all New Age enthusiasts are pantheists in the strictest sense. Not everyone associated with the movement agrees with all New Age elements presented here, at least not to the same degree. Each New Age enthusiast lives with the assumptions, beliefs, and practices of the movement in an individualized way. Some view the role of the Divine in a way that reflects Christian notions of creation and grace; Christianity and the New Age do not always hold absolutely different perspectives. Because official Church teachings state that Christian faith and strict pantheism are incompatible, no Catholic who is sympathetic to New Age beliefs and practices should knowingly accept the basic principles of pantheism.

*If some elements of pantheistic belief can help us better appreciate everyone and everything, is it still shortsighted to think that through divine power we can have special influence on other people and things?*

One characteristic of New Age belief is the notion that the reality or situation known to us is often more a product of our mentality and consciousness than something we know rather passively. *Thought* is primarily a disposition that causes what is known. For example, if I enjoy good relationships at home and am productive at work, this is primarily because I see myself this way. My positive attitudes about my interpersonal and professional skills have preceded my successes and are factors that have contributed to them; I do not simply come to know passively that I am successful at home or work. Many New Age followers speak of the influence of thought on reality as "mind over matter." This influence, they say, is partially due to the effect of positive attitudes and heightened consciousness on behavior and accomplishments.

This relationship between thought and reality is a major element of the contemporary psychological methodology known as cognitive therapy. The New Age appreciates this approach to personal change and self-realization. But the issue of mind over matter also involves, as the New Age suggests, the inherent power that all persons possess to affect change both within and outside of themselves. Divine energy that all people share explains this power partially. The mind's capacity to influence reality is sacred and, according to the New Age, must not be abused. Rather, it must be used responsibly for the good of all.

Catholics, like many other Christians, believe in the special value of prayers of petition when persons of faith make hopeful requests to God. The desired outcomes, if they are truly good for all concerned, can be viewed as God's loving and gracious response. The power of prayer, though considered real, is clearly not identical to the New Age concept that prayer is a built-in divine capacity to effect change. In the Christian view, God is the direct cause of a prayed-for change. The most apparent similarity between mind over matter and the prayer of petition is the personal thought that in both instances initiates a process of change.

Christians are also comfortable with biblical teachings regarding a link between personal human intention and a desired outcome. Biblical understanding of this connection resembles the New Age view of thought as a determinant of a reality already known. The Book of Sirach, demonstrating its familiarity with the power of thought, notes: "The mind is the root of all conduct" (Sirach 37:17). The gospels show Jesus giving his disciples extraordinary capacities, including the power to heal (Luke 9:1). Paul observes that such powers also come to the Christian from the Holy Spirit (1 Corinthians 12:9-10). In each instance these powers are used by persons whose minds and hearts are set on God and have been transformed by a faith receptive to divine wisdom and grace.

*Is trust in personal divine capacities what leads devotees of the New Age to have so much confidence in psychic and paranormal powers?*

For hundreds, even thousands of years, people of almost every culture and race have experienced an awareness not dependent upon the five senses or deductive reasoning processes. This awareness and knowledge has been explained as an intuition that allows people to be in touch with their worlds through extraordinary techniques: telepathy, clairvoyance, and precognition. Telepathy is a type of mind-to-mind communication. Through clairvoyance persons know the nature or significance of something of which they have had no immediate sensory experience. Precognition includes the ability to predict the future through fortunetelling and other methods. Psychokinesis is a related phenomenon involving a perceived ability to influence or maneuver physical objects through mental disposition.

These and similar abilities have been used in various societies for self-improvement and for helping others. The Gospels say Jesus drew on his knowledge of others' thoughts to challenge their narrow ways of thinking (Luke 5:22; 6:8; 9:47; 11:17) and to forgive (Luke 7:39,47-48). The Bible mentions precognition in the form of divinely inspired prophecy as a gift granted both to Israel and the Church. With some exceptions, as when extraordinary capacities like prophecy and healing are appreciated as "charismatic gifts," Christian attention to paranormal powers has waned in recent centuries. Though admitting that God is able to reveal the future through prophecy, the *Catechism of the Catholic Church* observes that trust in God's providence should replace "all unhealthy curiosity" about the future (2115).

### Does the Bible condemn such things like fortunetelling and other paranormal activities?

The Bible's position on many subjects, including fortunetelling, is not stated definitively. Indeed Deuteronomy directs some harsh words against clairvoyance and precognition in the forms of divination (seeing the future in signs and omens), soothsaying (prediction through magic), and prophecy (prediction through divine inspiration) (Deuteronomy 18:9-14,20). But the judgment warns against activities which have not been integrated into Israel's faith. In several places the Bible speaks acceptingly and even positively of fortunetelling, especially when it serves as a kind of prophecy (Genesis 44:4-5; Deuteronomy 18:15; Sirach 48:24; Acts of the Apostles 19:6).

Elsewhere, methods associated with the paranormal, like the casting of lots, are accepted without question (Joshua 18:10; 1 Samuel 28:6; Luke 1:9; Acts of the Apostles 1:26). Since these procedures ultimately depend on divine power for their effectiveness (Proverbs 16:33), they should be trusted only when they come from God (Sirach 34:5-6). Reliance on psychic or paranormal powers, like a modern Christian's use of prayer techniques from non-Christian religions, must serve authentic faith. A Christian's relationship to God should be understood in terms of creation and grace, not in terms of pantheism. Nevertheless, because of its viewpoint that these kinds of techniques currently conceal superstitious and irreligious attitudes, the *Catechism of the Catholic Church* teaches that all divination, false precognition, "interpretation of omens and lots," and clairvoyance "are to be rejected" (2116).

Many in the New Age movement find inspiration in the paranormal. Their sense of how it works does not need to be directly connected with a pantheistic view of reality. They seem to presume that a person's extrasensory knowledge or nonphysical influence on reality depends on some kind of connection among all things. The New Age thus responds quite positively to the findings of some contemporary scientists like physicists and biologists who say that many of the extraordinary properties of matter and nature are explainable by a universal unifying factor. While the full identification of this factor is still unknown and disputed, some scientists think that it possesses the characteristics of a mind, exhibits signs of life, or has a spiritual nature. The psychologist Carl Jung thought that all humanity is bound together by a "collective unconscious," a kind of psychic storehouse of common human insights and dispositions. Such a unifying factor could help explain the paranormal connection between minds, as well as an individual's mental ability to influence or maneuver physical objects.

Some ancient Greeks believed that the harmony of the universe ensues from a divinely issued power or "word" (*logos*) that penetrates all things. Borrowing this idea, as well as the traditional Jewish notion of divine creative wisdom, New Testament writers depict Christ as the Word of God, the One in whom all things exist and come to their perfection (John 1:1-4; Colossians 1:15-20). Christians' ability to work miracles, Paul says, is related to their faith in this Christ (1 Corinthians 12:3-11).

### Do instruments like tarot cards really work?

If the casting of lots can indicate God's intentions, perhaps because of the unity of all things in Christ, then theoretically so can cards designed for fortunetelling. Many proponents of the New Age are convinced that a reading of the cards, whose symbolism is often aligned with ancient mythologies and structures of the unconscious mind, provides a means of assessing human spiritual potential. However, no biblical evidence states that these kinds of prophecies are reliable, and Catholic theology and spirituality have not recognized the validity of the tarot deck. Catholics have often sought divine guidance through various tangible directives; some prayerfully yet randomly open the Bible and spontaneously point to a verse that they expect will convey a message appropriate to the moment. Saint Bonaventure recounts that Saint Francis of Assisi was able to confirm the religious vocation of one of his first followers when the Gospels opened three consecutive times to related texts.

# THREE

*Nature, Crystals,
and the Stars*

*Is belief in the oneness of all things related to New Age concern for
the environment?*

Some contemporary scientists say that all life on our planet is so inter-
connected that earth functions as one living organism. All life-support systems support one another as the circulatory, digestive, and other systems
work together for the body's health and survival. Earth's soil, water, air,
foliage, and animal life are major components of a finely tuned ecology and
life system that maintains and fosters the planet's health and well-being.
Humans affect this ecology positively and negatively, individually and col-
lectively, consciously and unconsciously. Many in the New Age movement,
sensitive to universal harmony, show great concern for the environment.
Human responsibilities, they believe, include respecting nature, protecting
all life forms, tending to ecological needs, and avoiding abuse through waste,
devastation, and pollution. Guarding and tending the planet is therefore
regarded as essential in serving the growth and health of all people. From
this perspective, personal dispositions toward environmental issues require careful examination and attention to solid scientific findings and also
to the insights and wisdom that flow from heightened consciousness and
spiritual growth.

The Catholic scholar Chardin, mentioned in Chapter One, proposed
that all life is unified through a movement toward fullness and completion
in Christ. This perspective accords with New Testament teachings regarding the universe's oneness in the divine Word. A vision of nature can,
therefore, be theological and include a Christian belief in the ways that
God attends to creation. The Book of Psalms repeatedly proclaims the

glory of God shining through the beauty of nature (65:6-13; 67:6-7; 96:10-13; 104; 147:7-9,16-18). Psalm 8 recalls that humanity enjoys a special relationship with the rest of God's creation (8:6-8). In the Book of Genesis, God gives newly created man and woman dominion over all life on earth (1:28). This charge, correctly understood, implies that humans must mirror God's own loving care for the world because they have been created in the divine image (1:27). The *Catechism of the Catholic Church* observes that this dominion, requiring responsible concern for both present and future generations, must manifest "a religious respect for the integrity of creation" (2415). Christians therefore, reminded of what has been entrusted to them, can join with the New Age in accepting responsibilities for their planet's health and beauty.

### Does the Bible share the New Age's special interest in certain elements of nature such as crystals?

For centuries, people have cherished crystals as agents of healing and wisdom, believing that their unique structure relates to the rest of nature in a way that directs various natural energies toward human life and undertakings. This belief presupposes the oneness of nature. From another perspective the sparkle of crystals symbolizes divine splendor. Many in the New Age share these kinds of reactions to precious stones. The properties of each kind of stone—there are hundreds of different kinds—depend on its type. New Age proponents believe that amber promotes relaxation and encourages good judgment, that diamonds improve self-esteem and foster insight, and that jade encourages peace and creativity. In addition, they believe that opal heightens love and joy while helping one maintain emotional balance, that white quartz confers healing power, and that turquoise makes people stronger and more communicative. Typically these stones are prepared and used according to established traditions. Many cultures consider the influence of stones particularly important for their leaders.

The Bible does not teach explicitly that jewels and crystals have such power, though Old Testament writers compare sapphire to heavenly clarity (Exodus 24:10) and associate the gem with divine radiance (Song of

Solomon 5:10,14). In addition, the Book of Isaiah associates this and other jewels with God's enduring love (54:10-12). Scripture clearly notes Israel's distinctive use of precious stones. The king of Israel wears a crown ornamented with a jewel (2 Samuel 12:30), and the high priest's breastplate contains twelve precious stones set in gold (Exodus 28:17-20). In the New Testament, various kinds of jewels comprise the heavenly Jerusalem's foundation (Revelation 21:19-20). According to biblical faith, all power and strength come ultimately from God and God's creation manifests divine glory and energy. We can surmise that the faith depicted in the Bible sensed the eminence of crystals as agents of sacred transforming energy.

Moving from biblical times to later centuries, we continue to find crystals used for spiritual and religious purposes. In Christian art a large jewel on a cross has symbolized Christ. And sapphires and other precious stones have adorned the rings of bishops and cardinals.

### Is New Age interest in astrology related to a belief in the powers of nature?

For centuries people have looked to the skies for guidance and direction for their lives. A complex system of aligning stars and interpreting movements of the planets has evolved into a methodology whereby the time and date of a person's birth can be used to describe that individual's personality, to tell that person's fortune, and to predict favorable and unfavorable times for making decisions. This practice of astrology has both avid enthusiasts and cynical opponents. Modern scientific assessments provide mixed conclusions. Some researchers see some relationship between a person's astrological birth sign (the stellar constellation in which a person's influencing planets are located) and that person's character traits.

Many in the New Age movement look to astrology for a way to designate a time when all humanity will experience heightened consciousness. Noting that the sun is moving toward the stellar constellation Aquarius, they associate the dawning age with this solar transition. Modern astronomy, the scientific study of the stars using current methodologies, observes that this transition is still centuries away. Nevertheless, the Age of Aquarius, some believe, is the favored time for which the New Age hopes.

The New Age movement involves interest in astrology primarily because proponents believe that stellar and planetary positions indicate personality strengths and weakness. When people have a general notion of their personalities and an idea of when crises and opportunities will occur, they can make appropriate decisions and design strategies for living. Thus the stars are regarded as helpful indicators, not infallible predictors.

Astrologers receive little mention in the Bible. In the Old Testament they appear as insignificant (Isaiah 47:13-14) or having questionable value (Daniel 1:20). Some evidence suggests that the gentile wise men in Matthew's account of Jesus' birth are astrologers. Though wise and honorable personalities, these dignitaries are subordinate to Jesus, the king of the Jews, whose star they have seen (Matthew 2:1-2).

Jewish and Christian spirituality in the Middle Ages included some astrological elements. Theology partially supported astrology's claims. Saint Thomas Aquinas argued eloquently that the stars and planets do indeed influence the physical elements of human existence but not to the extent that this influence interferes with human choices and the operations of free will. Popes consulted their astrologers. The seven days of the week, even on the Church calendar, have astrological roots. Nevertheless, recent Catholic theology has taken a conservative position when assessing astrology. In the sixteenth and seventeenth centuries popes condemned it mainly because of the dire effects that predictions would have on society. The *Catechism of the Catholic Church*, finding astrology superstitious and irreligious, says it should be rejected (2116). In modern times the prudent Catholic will distinguish between amusement from journalistic astrology and serious faith in a system whose foundations are questionable.

### Does an appreciation of nature's powers affect the New Age interest in herbs and natural essences?

These products from nature serve in New Age circles as medicines or folk remedies. Generations of experimentation and a heritage of healing techniques among many peoples, including the ancient Chinese, have contributed to the current collections of recipes accepted as agents of strength, health, and revitalization. Careful experimentation according to modern scientific methods also gives credibility to the use of healing essences extracted from herbs and other plants. These prescriptions, whether ancient or modern, are sniffed, taken internally, or applied appropriately to the body. As the prime ingredients of aroma therapy and herbal healing, they are directed toward physical health as well as an inducement to the higher consciousness so dear to the New Age. In both instances they are said to serve healing and holistic growth through appreciating human existence as a whole and through fostering the beneficial influence of body, mind, and spirit on one another. Therefore, the therapeutic use of natural extracts is often combined with other healthful techniques like relaxation, massage, dieting, positive thinking, meditation, and prayer.

Herbal and aroma therapies, as well as other forms of "alternative medicine," have historically faced resistance from medical doctors, professional organizations, and governmental agencies. Concerns have been more about the ineffectiveness of these therapies rather than immediate danger to the user. Increased appreciation of holistic approaches to health, both in society generally and among scientists, has resulted in a considerable diminishing of these concerns though caution still prevails. The highly reputable American Holistic Medical Association, emphasizing attention to the wholesome interdependence of body, mind, and spirit, includes unconventional therapies in programs for healing and maintaining good health. Catholic ethical teachings accept and even encourage the prudent and appropriate use of all established and reliable therapies. Catholics are not forbidden to utilize New Age and other alternative approaches to health as long as these have only good purposes and clearly involve no unreasonable risk, harm, or wrongdoing. In questionable circumstances, Catholics are encouraged to seek guidance from competent medical and spiritual advisors.

The Bible gives little explicit advice regarding natural healing agents. According to John's Gospel, Jesus once applied mud to the eyes of a blind man who then immediately began to see (9:6-7). While John clearly connects the mud with the restoration of sight (9:14), he also mentions Jesus' saliva used to make the mud (9:6) and the water from the Siloam pool with which the man immediately washed himself (9:11). Ancient peoples believed spittle possessed protective and healing power. Although the Bible usually describes spitting as an insult (Numbers 12:14; Job 30:10; Mark 14:65), Mark shows Jesus using spittle to heal dumbness (7:33) and, combined with touch, to heal blindness (8:23). In a similar manner the ancient Church used spittle in baptism, demonstrating that Satan, with his corrupting influence on the senses, was being dispelled.

The importance of water in the baptismal rite of initiation illustrates the Christian use of natural elements in sacramental and symbolic ways rather than as medicinal agents. Water was commonly thought among many ancient peoples, including the Israelites, to manifest purifying and regenerative power. For Paul and his communities, water symbolizes both the earth from which the baptized person rises spiritually transformed (Romans 6:4) and an agent of spiritual cleansing (Ephesians 5:26-27). Echoing ancient customs, Catholics today use holy water in blessings and prayer.

We observe additional Christian uses of other elements like salt and oil; Catholics believe their power comes more from divine influence rather than solely from their inherent capacities. Able to both preserve foods and enhance flavors, salt has historically and in various cultures been prized for its power to protect people from evil and to connect them with divine life and wisdom. Christians, Jesus says, are "salt of the earth" (Matthew 5:13). Paul adds that the gracious and proper words of Christians should be "seasoned with salt" (Colossians 4:6). Fittingly then, this seasoning is touched to the lips of those receiving baptism. *The Roman Ritual*, used for hundreds of years in the Catholic Church before Vatican II, contained a blessing for salt that could be used for healing dog bites. Today some Catholics bring salt to their churches to have it blessed for use at the table.

Oil, commonly extracted from olives, is an element widely used in healing, blessings, anointings, and consecrations. Mark reports in his gospel that the apostles "anointed with oil many who were sick and cured them" (6:13). Symbolizing grace and the Holy Spirit, oil is used in several sacraments, including baptism, confirmation, and ordination. When blessing the oil used in the anointing of the sick, the priest prays that the power of the Holy Spirit will enter the ointment and make it a remedy for physical, psychological, and spiritual afflictions.

# FOUR

# *Health, Healing, and Reincarnation*

*What more can be said about holistic health?*

Typically, we associate health with the body and its biological characteristics and functions. The New Age, however, carefully observes that bodily and physical existence is but a single part of one reality which also includes emotional, mental, psychological, and spiritual components. The terms *body, mind,* and *spirit* are used together to designate the coordinated aspects of human existence. According to this view, health is incomplete unless all these elements are working for an individual's fitness and vitality. A pantheistic view of reality, which regards all as one with divine goodness, helps the New Age devotee believe that everyone is naturally disposed toward good health. This view, reflecting a confident attitude and a positive disposition of the mind, does much to influence total health, including body and spirit. Confidence of this kind is another feature of the higher consciousness so valued by the New Age.

But the natural disposition toward health, the New Age also believes, can be interrupted and disturbed by neglecting any of the elements of body, mind, and spirit or by introducing into them any kind of negativity. Thus negative thoughts can harm the body; for example, worry often causes stomach ulcers. Sinful habits also take their toll. Similarly, lack of physical exercise leads to mental sluggishness. Lack of self-control, a disposition of the mind and will, leads to spiritual and moral decadence.

Total well-being, the New Age says, requires careful and positive attention to each of these areas. From this holistic perspective, a nutritious and well-balanced diet (caring for the body), dedicated study (developing the mind), and fervent prayer (nurturing the spirit) contribute to maintaining or regaining good health. They affect our total well-being while influencing one another. The New Age, however, does not claim to have found the secret of unending perfect health. Higher consciousness, for example, does not guarantee a robust and disease-free condition. The advanced awareness may only be partial; the undeveloped parts of consciousness remain to negatively affect other areas of health, perhaps in the body, thereby causing weakness or illness.

Through its holistic approach to health, the New Age shares much with practitioners from other eras and cultures who have relied on an advantageous combination of physical care, psychological influence, and spiritual power to induce or preserve good health. Some cultures call these healers *shamans* or *medicine men.* Contemporary science shows increased interest in shamanistic artistry and skill. In countries like the United States, where populations include people of different cultures, increasing numbers of physicians welcome the participation of native and folk healers in medical treatment. Among some Hispanic Catholics, many techniques of traditional healers, or *curanderos,* are still highly regarded. Catholic pastoral teachings concerning the care of the sick and dying enthusiastically endorse reputable holistic approaches to health. Clearly, trickery and recourse to "evil powers" should have no place here (*Catechism of the Catholic Church,* 2117). The *Introduction to the Rite of Anointing and the Pastoral Care of the Sick* notes that the sacrament of anointing "gives to the sick person the grace of the Holy Spirit by which the whole person is made healthy....Restoration to health may follow the reception of the sacrament if this will be in the interests of the sick person's salvation" (6).

The Bible emphasizes the spiritual aspect of healing. Through the power of God, Christ, and the Holy Spirit, people may be cured, rejuvenated, and even restored to life. Such power is often manifested through a believer's influence, as when Elijah prays for the revival of the widow's son (1 Kings 17:22), when Peter commands the paralytic to stand up (Acts of the Apostles 9:34), and when a Christian relies on the spiritual gifts of healing (1 Corinthians 12:9,30). But the divine power to heal is also manifested through the faith of the one healed, like the hemorrhaging woman cured by Jesus (Mark 5:34), the lame man cured by Peter (Acts of the

Apostles 3:16), and the crippled man cured by Paul (Acts of the Apostles 14:9-10). In each instance the healer identifies the sufferer's faith as an agent of the cure.

Without underestimating this spiritual emphasis on healing, we find biblical support for respecting human intervention in effecting physical cures: Jesus suggests that physicians are necessary (Luke 5:31). Such appreciation accords well with the views of Ben Sira; this Old Testament sage considers the physician an honorable healer whose diagnosis, skills, and medicines are gifts from God (Sirach 38:1-8,12-14). Yet Ben Sira's view of health is definitely holistic; he advises those who commit themselves to physicians to also pray for healing, redirect their lives away from sin, and offer generous sacrifice (Sirach 38:9-11). These prescriptions for body and spirit are complemented by his counsel that speech be pleasant and constructive, leading to wholesomeness of thought and mind (Sirach 37:16-18); attitudes of mind affect emotions that, when positive, contribute to good health and lengthen one's life (Sirach 30:16,22,25). For divine wisdom to be wholly beneficial, therefore, we must guard against negative dispositions like worry, jealousy, and undue anger (Sirach 30:17,21,23-24). These harmful dispositions inhibit physical, mental, and spiritual health.

### Does this mean, according to the Bible or the New Age, that sickness and suffering are forms of punishment?

The biblical view of health is that personal choices often affect the circumstances of our lives. Good choices regarding attention to the body, orientation of the mind, and direction of the spirit work for our well-being, health, and happiness. In a parallel manner poor, incorrect, and immoral choices regarding any part of our being work negatively and may bring illness, pain, and even death. From one perspective the negative outcomes are self-inflicted. But the Bible offers another perspective when it speaks of afflictions as punishments from God (2 Samuel 24:15; Psalm 39:11). Jesus shares this view (Matthew 9:2; John 5:14). The Bible's association of the consequences of good and bad acts as either reward or punishment is often called the doctrine of retribution. Virtue is rewarded; wrongdoing is punished.

But this teaching leaves the issue unresolved. The Bible also emphasizes that immoral or evil persons may experience no punishment, at least temporarily. Furthermore, the good and innocent often suffer, usually for reasons known only to God. Psalm 73 compellingly presents these considerations. Jesus' teachings indicate that he also shared similar views (Luke 13:1-5; John 9:1-3). The biblical accounts of the lives of Job and Jesus are powerful instructions in both the validity and limits of the doctrine of retribution. A basically good man whose afflictions seem grossly disproportionate to his just deserts, Job attains new intimacy with God and is brought by divine blessings to new joys of spiritual, familial, civic, and economic life. Jesus is sinless. Moreover he is filled with the Spirit of God and overflows with divine compassion. Yet he suffers the indignities of rejection during his ministry and is eventually crucified. His ultimate destiny, however, is resurrection and heavenly glory.

The New Age is rather comfortable with joy and sorrow as consequences of personal decisions and a chosen lifestyle. Interest in holistic health and trust in the power of heightened consciousness fit securely within a frame of reference that accepts the doctrine of retribution. Many in the New Age movement seem to have little room, however, for divinely-sanctioned illness and sorrow in an innocent and virtuous person's life. They accept afflictions as something to endure or reform before attaining greater heights of joy. These afflictions, they say, ensue either automatically as the natural consequences of certain dispositions or from purposeful action, such as painful self-sacrifice which moves us beyond the imperfections of selfishness. From this perspective, we have only ourselves to blame for our problems, sorrows, and pain. We reap what we sow. No one else is responsible. Every sick and sorrowing person is thus challenged to look within and ask, "How should I change?" Since we tend to look for the primary cause of problems in the wrong place, usually in others' attitudes and actions or in external agents like germs and viruses, we see the wisdom of this self-examination.

Similar reasons prompt Catholics to admit their failings through prayer to God or to participate in the spiritual action of sacramental reconciliation, not confessing others' faults but acknowledging their own weaknesses and sins. This confession allows them in a dynamic way to accept personal responsibility for certain undesirable features of their lives and to trust with spiritual vigor that God's forgiving grace will sustain them on a journey toward greater peace and blessedness.

Connecting illness and affliction with wrong choices thus has advantages. From both biblical and New Age perspectives, we can recognize our faults as roots of problems and take steps to improve our behavior accordingly. We must be careful, however, not to assume needless guilt if we have done little or nothing to cause or provoke a dreadful situation; our afflictions—disease or loss, for example—can be unrelated to our actions. Falsely believing that we are responsible for the distress only multiplies difficulties, especially if our attempts to change behaviors or attitudes do nothing to alleviate pain or hardship. Frustration and groundless guilt just make matters worse.

The Bible's broader view of the mystery of suffering allows people to accept pain and sorrow as part of God's will, even when it is unexplainable and appears to be unjust. Trusting in God's overwhelming mercy, Christians wait for recompense according to a mysterious and grand design, associating their plight with Christ's suffering, assured that through his cross their sorrow has meaning (Colossians 1:24). They know through faith that all things, even unexplainable sickness and suffering, "work together for good for those who love God, who are called according to his purpose" (Romans 8:28). For even in the midst of terminal illness, Christians confidently anticipate that, forgiven and redeemed, they will experience heavenly joys and be transformed through glorious resurrection.

The New Age's apparently stricter association of destiny with personal choice influences the way many in the movement understand the significance of death. If termination of earthly life, they say, interrupts development toward wholeness of body, mind, and spirit, then there is still work to do and a higher consciousness to achieve. In such a case, death for the New Age begins a transition to another earthly existence and another life, possibly in another age and place. This change is known as reincarnation.

**Does the New Age belief in reincarnation mean that one will never depart from earthly existence?**

The New Age concept of a new earthly life after death is primarily adapted from the teachings of Hinduism and Buddhism. Here New Age enthusiasts share much in common with millions of others, especially non-Western peoples, from ancient times to the present. The goal of personal existence is to attain the highest level of consciousness and thus achieve fullness of being when the unity of body, mind, and spirit makes these three elements indistinguishable from one another. In pantheistic terms all aspects of the person or consciousness have fully realized their divine essence, becoming so absorbed into it that all is now present as divinity or God with no illusion of separateness. At this point, according to those who profess this belief, one realizes with utter clarity that one is not merely an individual human being among others, but is the divinity, is God; that is all there is. Others in the New Age movement believe that they may attain a level of godly perfection without becoming pure divinity.

Such goals are considered unattainable during a single lifetime. Too much ignorance, too many illusions, and too much selfishness obstruct the path. Too many failures, the consequences of trial and error, retard progress. Ordinarily the process of total self-realization takes many earthly lifetimes, perhaps hundreds or even thousands of them. Each phase of earthly existence ends with death, but only for the body. The enduring but departed essence or soul, as mind and spirit, enters into a new body, reincarnates itself, and begins a new human life. Often the transition from one body to another does not occur instantaneously but is delayed by a pause in a supernatural realm or dimension until the soul is ready for reincarnation. The type of body to enter or the new life to be assumed is sometimes believed to be a matter for personal choice.

The speed with which the soul, progressing through a chain of reincarnations, reaches its ultimate destiny or reward depends on the kinds of decisions, activities, and accomplishments of each individual lifetime. The deeds and occupations must engage the whole person: body, mind, and spirit. Profitable acts and habits like charity, study, and prayer hasten the process. Pernicious acts and habits like abuse, laziness, and blasphemy impede it. The better a person is in the present life, the higher that person's consciousness or development will be in the next. Correspondingly, decadence and immorality lead to a lower-level existence, perhaps even animal life, in the next phase. Therefore, progress toward salvation as undistorted oneness in divinity can, according to the belief, not only be accelerated or decelerated but can also be temporarily stopped or reversed. Eventually the soul, prompted by its inherently divine capacities, will attain salvation.

At least two biblical teachings, namely those regarding retribution and forgiveness, can be linked to the notion of reincarnation. The Bible's concept that reward and punishment correspond to a believer's merit and demerit aligns with the New Age notion that personal choices influence progress and regression. The biblical proclamation of divine forgiveness that allows for renewed spiritual headway after failure is similar to the New Age's confidence in divine capacities that allow multiple opportunities for growth in consciousness to recur through reincarnation.

The major difference between the biblical and New Age notions of reincarnation revolves around the implications of a person's death. The Epistle to the Hebrews says, "It is appointed for mortals to die once, and after that the judgment" (9:27). Generally, biblical authors appear to assume that a person lives only one life on this earth. Yet the earthly and bodily presence of those who have given up their physical forms through death is also accepted. The Gospels reveal that Jesus' contemporaries thought that he might be John the Baptist, Elijah, or some other prophet returned to life (Luke 9:7-8). Belief in the possibility of reappearance seems confirmed by various gospel accounts of persons who rise from the dead, including the widow's son (Luke 7:12-15) and Lazarus (John 11:43-44). According to Matthew, after Jesus' death a number of holy persons came back from their graves and appeared in Jerusalem (27:52-53).

Jesus' own Resurrection and subsequent appearances to the early Christians also confirm the biblical belief that presence on earth is not definitively discontinued by death. Jesus' return to life is unique, however: he, crucified and risen, brings salvation to the world (1 Corinthians 15:17; Colossians 1:18-20). Moreover, his new life entails arrival at heavenly glory

(John 17:5; 1 Corinthians 15:42-47) and is the sign of the heavenly existence that believers can attain (1 Corinthians 15:49). Whether speaking of Jesus or others, the Bible depicts resurrection as reembodiment—new life in which the body is transformed for immortality. Some might consider resurrection a form of reincarnation. But this reincarnation as a single occurrence is clearly distinguished from reincarnation in the New Age sense: embodiment repeated over many earthly lifetimes.

### Does the idea of reincarnation mean salvation is hopelessly out of reach?

For those who believe in reincarnation, earthly existence indicates incompleteness, lack of resolution, and an unfulfilled need for perfect happiness. Bad decisions made during one life lead to reincarnation and continue to be problematic until their influence is overcome. The pain and struggle of human existence have, in the Catholic tradition, led to life's being called a "valley of tears." In the context of prayer, this description is not a cry of despair or bitterness, but a sigh of acceptance. Recognizing that life is frequently bittersweet becomes part of the Catholic hope in the divine comfort and support that adds wondrous sweetness. John the Baptist proclaims that "the kingdom of heaven has come near" (Matthew 3:2) and thus reassures those who are properly disposed that life offers a foretaste of eternal blessedness. The New Age also professes that higher consciousness, even if not the highest, offers a rewarding sense of divinity's nearness.

Nevertheless, because of limited, negative, and immoral choices made in a previous life, a person's degree of consciousness or self-realization is less than is possible and thus remains a problem. In this sense, many in the New Age movement say, people "suffer" the consequences of past decisions. But suffering can provide opportunities to learn and grow. For example, suffering may teach what changes are required to become a more enlightened or better person. Suffering thus serves a process of refinement. Some New Age enthusiasts even hold that the dead, as spirits, may choose a reincarnation characterized by serviceable forms of suffering. Some psychotherapists, utilizing their clients' belief in reincarnation, encourage images of past lives and then explore these perceptions as an aid in healing. Instead of making salvation seem distant, afflictions inspire hope that salvation will be attained more quickly.

Similarly, the Bible teaches that suffering marks a life of faith and hope (Sirach 2:1-6). Even Jesus faced the challenge of suffering and responded by obeying his heavenly Father (Mark 14:36; Hebrews 5:8). Sirach says that afflictions and humiliations prepare the faithful person for God the way "gold is tested in the fire" (2:5). Jeremiah also uses this image of the refining and purifying power of suffering (9:7).

Suffering required for refinement, purification, and purging of undesirable qualities therefore delays salvation, but in a way that facilitates its attainment. Appreciation of this principle and the application of it to life after death characterize not only the New Age notion of reincarnation, but also the traditional Catholic belief in purgatory. For centuries the Church, sensitive to the endurance usually required for perfect sanctity, has offered much insight on the path of human spiritual growth. The Church believes that the ultimate enjoyment of heavenly blessedness may require a period of refinement after death if during earthly life a person made insufficient restitution for sins and demonstrated insufficient love for God and neighbor. This period, marked by the same kind of hope that God's grace sustains on earth, can be envisioned as a positive time in which "the kingdom of heaven has come near," perhaps nearer to those in purgatory than to many persons on earth. The basic healing of the believer still dwelling on this side of death occurs through the graces of redemption and conversion, a healing and salvation that comes through faith and baptism and that sustains us in the hope of eternal risen life. Yet the possibility remains that this hope is not fully realized until after death. Catholics therefore pray that their dead may enjoy heavenly peace and perpetual light.

*If, according to Church teaching, spiritual growth can occur after death as well as in this life, could someone's purgatory after dying be here on earth if that person reincarnates?*

The *Catechism of the Catholic Church* disclaims the existence of reincarnation as an individual's repetition of earthly lifetimes (1013). Surely life in this "valley of tears" sometimes resembles a kind of purgatory. Though proclaiming that through Christ we participate in heavenly holiness here on earth, Vatican II's *Dogmatic Constitution on the Church* also notes the trials of the present. Because history is not yet completed by Christ's Second Coming, the world and the Church still "groan and travail" (48). In the Catholic tradition, however, no precedent exists for believing in reincarnation. When Vatican II speaks of those "who are yet being purified after their death," it in no way suggests that the "living communion" (51) with them is enjoyed in the same way as with those who still live among us. Prayer for the dead in purgatory and fellowship with them through oneness in Christ are not equated with the bonds that exist between those still living on earth.

# FIVE

# *The World of Spirits*

**What do proponents of New Age practices think of Catholics' praying for the dead?**

With their convictions regarding paranormal knowledge and influence, many in the New Age movement appreciate these prayers as effective forms of benevolence and compassion toward someone who has completed a given incarnation or earthly life. They understand the prayer more as directing divine energy rather than asking God to grant grace and mercy to the deceased. Moreover, their belief in reincarnation permits them to remain undecided about whether the departed soul exists beyond our earthly domain or has assumed a new body somewhere among us. By New Age standards, the Catholic practice of praying for the dead is also an occasion for communicating with someone who once lived on earth. Catholics, of course, believe that a departed person, whether in purgatory or heaven, hears the prayers of others. Catholics pray to Christ, the divine Son who intercedes for them with the heavenly Father (Romans 8:34; Hebrews 7:25). They also pray to Mary and multitudes of saints, asking them to intercede with God. Such practice, along with intercession for souls in purgatory, demonstrates community and mutual support within the Body of Christ.

Throughout church history, Christians have experienced what they understand to be communications from beyond this life. Visions, voices, and dreams have led many to report that they have met Jesus, Mary, and departed loved ones. Though the Catholic Church officially confirms these experiences infrequently, tradition regards them as possibilities for revealing God's loving designs for this world. The *Catechism of the Catholic Church* teaches that revelations of this kind do not "improve or complete Christ's definitive Revelation, but...help live more fully by it in a certain period of history" (67). Many devotees of the New Age believe in spiritualism and are comfortable with and even welcome communication with the dead.

### Does spiritualism mean that at will we can have two-way interaction with anyone who has died?

For centuries many cultures throughout the world have regarded consulting with the dead a beneficial practice, especially for regaining health and growing in wisdom. In these traditions departed spirits are loving personalities whose resources are available to help those still struggling on earth. This esteem, however, is granted only to those spirits considered benevolent. Malicious and destructive spirits must be feared and avoided. Similar dispositions prevail in the kinds of present-day spiritualism in which the New Age shows interest. New Age proponents believe that God or divine presence protects the consulting parties from evil spirits' harm. It is difficult to confirm scientifically whether spiritualism works as it claims or whether it merely manifests a practitioner's psychological state. Trickery, of course, falsifies spiritualism's claims.

Séances, or spiritualist consultations, are typically led by someone believed to be a medium, the person through whom the spirit is expected to communicate with those present. In the technique of channeling, the medium is thought to be chosen by the departed spirit. The spirit is believed to bring useful messages to the present world through the voice, mannerisms, or writings of the medium. Sometimes the medium simply claims to receive the spirit's messages mentally and then relates the supposed message. Or the medium may, in a darkened room, speak through a megaphone or facilitate a sense that the spirit is communicating directly through this kind of device. Communication through automatic writing is said to occur when a spirit influences the medium to set pen to paper.

In some instances, participants in séances claim to experience, through the medium's direction, a visible manifestation of the spirit. Other variations on these spiritualist techniques are claimed to promote interaction with a specific spirit chosen by the participants. Typically the communications that appear to come from the spirit seem designed to help the participants, offering consolation, hope, and philosophically sound directives for wholesome and happy living. Sometimes either the medium, the participants, or both explicitly invoke divine assistance in barring evil influences from the séance.

## Should Catholics participate in spiritualist activities?

The Bible offers both positive and negative perspectives on communicating with the dead. A conversation between Israel's King Saul and the dead prophet Samuel occurs with the assistance of a medium. Though questioning why he was disturbed, Samuel confirms God's designs for Saul (1 Samuel 28:11-17) in accord with one pattern through which departed spirits were expected to speak: "From the ground like the voice of a ghost" (Isaiah 29:4). The gospel accounts of Jesus' Transfiguration depict him speaking with two Old Testament prophets, Moses and Elijah; these prophets also appear to the disciples who are present (Mark 9:2-4). Luke notes explicitly the prophets "appeared in glory" (9:31) with heavenly brilliance.

On the other hand the Book of Deuteronomy forbids the practice of spiritualism (18:11). We need to understand that this precept was a safeguard against rituals connected with the worship of alien gods. Yahweh commanded the Israelites to be "completely loyal" to their God (18:13), forbidding them to offer sacrifice to the dead (26:14). Israel was also reminded not to "consult the ghosts and the familiar spirits" as if these spirits were gods, for only God should be regarded as holy (Isaiah 8:13, 19-20).

According to Jewish and Christian teachings, only God is holy in the strictest sense. Through God's blessings and grace, however, those who believe in and love him become a holy people. The Christian belief in the communion of saints accepts that those who comprise the church community, both the living and the dead, share in this holiness. This means, according to Catholic teaching, that the union of all—on earth, in purgatory, and in heaven—is "reinforced by an exchange of spiritual goods" (*Dogmatic Constitution on the Church*, 49). Pope Paul VI's *The Credo of the People of God* states that "in this communion we are surrounded by the love and compassion of God and his saints, who always listen to our prayers."

In principle, Catholic teaching is not opposed to appropriate forms of association between the living and the dead. In practice, the recommended forms of interaction with the dead are mostly limited to prayer on behalf of those in purgatory and requests for intercession by those in heaven. Since 1856 the Vatican has forbidden participation in spiritism or spiritualist activities because of the potential for physical and moral harm caused by encounters with malicious spirits. The *Catechism of the Catholic Church* says the Church "warns the faithful" against spiritism (2117). Scientific investigations of it, however, are not prohibited.

### Has the New Age movement gained any recognition from science?

Much of what the New Age stands for can be considered a reaction to science, at least to the kind that prevailed until the early twentieth century. With its focus upon investigation and experimentation in the realm of the physical and measurable, modern science has made outstanding contributions toward understanding and improving our world. At the same time, and contrary to the best intentions of most scientists, emphasis on material reality has contributed to a general sense among many people that the spiritual realm is unimportant. Religion has often been unsuccessful in countering these kinds of attitudes, despite its attempt to help persons find meaningful and beneficial associations with God or the spiritual realm. Hence one way to view the New Age movement is as an alternative that helps people fulfill spiritual needs.

Recent generations of scientists, however, have devoted much reasoning, research, and experimentation to demonstrating that the traditional scientific view of reality has been too narrow. In the newer, contemporary scientific methodologies there is room for the spiritual domain and even a welcoming of it as an essential factor for understanding the world, nature, and life itself. New physics, for example, proposes that material reality has many features at variance with the laws of traditional physics. These features, some scientists say, point to the existence of a fundamental dimension or order in which all reality is enfolded. And this order resembles what has been referred to elsewhere as God or the divine. Moving into the spiritual dimension, science gives credibility to the New Age movement and some established religions, acknowledgements not typically granted by traditional science.

Science's other affirmations of New Age interests are found in theories related to subatomic structures and black holes. Within these frames of reference, science helps validate belief in phenomena like time travel and instantaneous movement from one physical domain to another. Moreover, several generations of scientists have given serious attention to people claiming psychic and paranormal powers. Though scientific findings vary and are inconclusive, scientists have not disproved all these claims. Science thus suggests that paranormal influence is more than coincidence and trickery.

Catholic theology has always been receptive to the valid insights of secular and nonreligious disciplines, for God creates human beings with intelligence that, combined with faith, provides reliable means for gaining heightened insight into the mysteries of God and God's creation. During past centuries collaboration was focused primarily in theology's attention to philosophical insights. More recently and with encouragement from Catholicism's official leadership, theological teachings have also increasingly been influenced by other disciplines: anthropology, psychology, medicine, and sociology. Vatican II's *Pastoral Constitution on the Church in the Modern World* teaches that such interaction helps Christians to be "brought to a purer and more mature living of the faith" (62). Catholic theology is thus better equipped to explore and evaluate more of contemporary life including the New Age movement. And when the New Age gains affirmations from contemporary science, Catholicism also develops its theological abilities to explore parts of its heritage like the paranormal power of prophecy and fortunetelling, which have not always been highly regarded in recent times.

### What other psychic or paranormal powers can Catholic theology consider?

One of the powers considered an example of mind over matter is psychokinesis, the ability to affect physical reality, including one's own body, through mental suggestion and energy. Where such power is perceived to have been exercised, it appears as a marvelous phenomenon. The Bible presents numerous examples of these occurrences. The patriarch Jacob uses striped rods to breed unusually colored livestock (Genesis 30:39-40). Because he mentally envisioned and directed the intended outcome, the incident can be regarded as an example of psychokinesis. Another prophet, Elijah, multiplies a poor widow's supply of meal and oil (1 Kings 17:14-16). The text, however, clearly indicates that the prophet's power comes from God.

Three Gospels mention that Jesus walked on water (Matthew 14:25; Mark 6:48; John 6:19). This feat could involve levitation; the body, through psychokinetic direction of the mind and will, floats in the air and defies gravitational force. Like the great figures of the Old Testament and the disciples to whom Jesus gives extraordinary powers (Matthew 10:1), Jesus may be said to enjoy psychokinetic power by divine design, though in a unique way. In Luke's account of the miraculous catch, mental energy that induces the large number of fish into the net can be the result of either Jesus' command (5:4) or of Simon's obedience (5:5). Though some biblical accounts are symbolic, the inspired authors appear to accept that descriptions of paranormal powers can be used to proclaim how God's work is accomplished.

Throughout the Catholic Church's history, many saints reportedly performed similar feats of psychokinesis. Official ecclesiastical teachings observe that a wondrous act can occur through God's direct and extraordinary intervention. But Church teachings also assume that some persons enjoy the use of preternatural gifts or wondrous, God-given capabilities through which marvels occur. In this manner Church teachings are sensitive to the existence of paranormal powers. Since the emergence of modern science, many Christians have been skeptical of and shown little interest in these kinds of powers. New Age interest in this subject, along with recent scientific advances, may entice Catholics and other Christians into a reexamination of this provocative dimension of the Church's heritage.

# SIX

## Dreams of Tonight and Tomorrow

*Is interpretation of dreams the same as spiritualism or fortunetelling?*

Throughout the world many people including numerous Catholics have experienced in dreams the presence of persons who have died. Sometimes the visitors in the dreams are in turmoil. Often the visitors bring messages of peace and assurances that death has led them to happiness. It is difficult to determine scientifically whether these dreams actually involve the departed personalities or are the results of the dreamers' unconscious creativity, but the dreamers consistently claim to have recognized actual personalities. These claims, to the extent that they are true, represent experiences we can call spiritualistic in a broad sense.

Other persons, again including Catholics, have experienced prophetic dreams, nocturnal visions of things to come. These kinds of dreams probably rely on the same paranormal powers active in precognition or prophecy during wakeful times. A third category of dreams includes those in which God is believed to be present. Comfort, healing, support, and blessings are often given to the dreamer. Here too it is difficult to determine with scientific and theological accuracy whether God actually entered the dream or whether the appearance symbolizes the believer's spiritual state or life of grace.

Many in the New Age movement rely on dreams as sources of paranormal knowledge like telepathy and precognition. Dreams are also used as symbols of the dreamer's personality and as guides to self-improvement and higher consciousness. The latter usage harmonizes with methodologies of modern psychology that frequently rely on dream interpretation for therapeutic purposes.

The Bible speaks frequently of dreams used as prophecy and as ways to receive messages from God. Joseph and the wise men are said to have experienced these kinds of dreams in connection with Jesus' birth (Matthew 1:20-2:22). According to biblical teachings, if the message of the dream is symbolic rather than explicit, it requires interpretation, a gift God gives to some individuals to help others understand the dream (Genesis 40:8). Not all dreams, however, are prophetic or of divine origin (Jeremiah 23:25). Therefore we can have confidence only in those dreams sent by God (Sirach 34:6). Dreams have played important roles throughout Christian history. Saint Helena is thought to have been led to the true cross of Jesus by a divinely inspired dream.

Working with dreams is usually a safe practice when dream stories and symbols are used in prayer and meditation; Catholic spirituality frequently utilizes dreams today. Interpreting images through God's help provides guidance for a better understanding of ourselves and our relationship to God. Formal instruction in dream interpretation, provided by ministers and other trained professionals, is usually required. These techniques can be learned on retreats, in workshops, and on days of reflection. Though it is possible for demonic or evil forces to manipulate the content of dreams, pastoral experience shows that the unwelcome presence of evil in dreams is unmistakable and rare. God seems to protect dreamers and to allow them to recognize malicious advice.

### New Age consciousness seems very individualistic. Does this have anything to do with relationships?

From New Age perspectives, heightened consciousness and greater happiness depend upon avoiding negative thoughts and enjoying positive ones; thoughts are intimately connected with feelings and behavior. Bitterness, resentment, and animosity reflect a preoccupation with wrongs inflicted upon us by others. On the other hand gentleness, composure, and goodwill flow from a grateful attitude toward others.

Viewed this way, New Age consciousness is individualistic because it emphasizes the importance of individuals' bettering their own lives, changing attitudes and behaviors that cause them unhappiness and pain. This is not a selfish individualism but an individualism considered indispensable for a love that will bring all humanity into greater harmony and peace. Universal love and altruism impels the New Age movement. Individuals are challenged to put their own houses in order so they can love and serve others, enfolding all humanity in the oneness of divine energy.

Christians need no reminder that universal love is also the heart of their religion. Jesus proclaims love of neighbor (Matthew 22:39) as one of the two great commandments of the Jewish law (Leviticus 20:1-17). His good Samaritan parable (Luke 10:29-37) is but one of many teachings regarding the command to love all persons, even enemies (Matthew 5:44). Surely service to others, compassion for the poor and marginalized, and dedication to social justice demonstrate the love that Jesus modeled. A love that transforms the world for the kingdom of God is necessarily communal. Yet Jesus also calls for repentance (Mark 1:15), conversion (Matthew 18:3), and self-sacrifice (Matthew 10:37-39). He challenges his followers to rid themselves of dispositions that interfere with loving human relationships (Matthew 5:22-24). He shows by his example that universal love begins with the individual. The New Age perceives love in the same way.

### Is this why forgiveness is so important in New Age spirituality?

An unforgiving heart bears burdens. Bitterness, resentment, and animosity are just a few of many negative dispositions associated with claims we make on others for what we perceive they owe us. When we demand payment, recompense, and justice from others, we are enslaved by the irritations that flow from these demands. Freedom from this captivity comes through letting go of our demands, acknowledging that others owe us nothing, and forgiving others completely and forever. For many New Age devotees, forgiveness is essential in attaining higher consciousness and wonderful peace.

Because the mind acts positively, refocusing thoughts and expectations, forgiveness serves as a therapeutic form of self-help. But forgiveness also involves acts of heart and will. According to the New Age holistic view, the unity of body, mind, and spirit allows forgiveness to be an eminently spiritual act. Releasing others from all indebtedness is thus regarded as a powerful way of opening oneself to greater love, to greater divine power, and thus to a greater sense of solidarity with all humanity. Because it allows divine energy to flow in a new way, forgiveness is a miracle of freedom and a key to true love.

The Bible proclaims forgiveness as one of the distinguishing features of God's relationship with humanity. For God is "merciful and gracious... abounding in steadfast love...forgiving iniquity and transgression and sin" (Exodus 34:6-7). Jesus taught that forgiving others is an important way of imitating God and enjoying the blessings and privileges given to God's children: "Love your enemies, do good, and lend, expecting nothing in return. Your reward will be great, and you will be children of the Most High; for he is kind to the ungrateful and the wicked. Be merciful, just as your Father is merciful" (Luke 6:35-36).

Jesus, following Old Testament tradition (Exodus 34:7), leaves no doubt that God is just and demands due recompense for offenses against divine decrees (Luke 11:51;12:48). A Christian, however, must avoid imitating this divine prerogative. "Vengeance is mine, I will repay, says the Lord" (Romans 12:19). Yet God abundantly complements divine justice with mercy. Jesus reminds his followers that they should forgive others even as they hope to experience the forgiving mercy of God (Luke 6:37-48). And so Christians pray, perhaps nervously, "Forgive us our trespasses as we forgive those who trespass against us."

### Is recompense or making amends—as in Alcoholics Anonymous—part of New Age spirituality?

To compensate for an offense against another is to demonstrate visibly and tangibly a change of mind and heart. At minimum this reparation expresses bodily, behaviorally, and sincerely the goodwill we have toward one another. When religious repentance accompanies benevolence and goodwill, perhaps reflecting a powerful and transforming awareness of divine justice and love, recompense promotes spiritual development. From a holistic perspective, making amends is essential to our transformation and healing if our affliction, addiction, disease, or vice has resulted in harm to others.

The healing elements listed by Alcoholics Anonymous and other twelve-step programs include admitting the harm we caused, desiring to make amends, and actually making amends when this causes no additional harm. Overcoming an addiction (whether to alcohol, food, narcotics, gambling, sex, or anything else) is considered a holistic process of healing. Body and mind, working together through reformed behavior and attitudes, cooperate with the spirit that seeks the transforming power of God or the Divine, however this being or power is understood by those seeking a new and healthier life.

Many associated with the New Age enthusiastically accept the twelve-step approach to personal transformation and growth. The holistic alignment of body, mind, and spirit harmonizes with New Age sentiments regarding health. The New Age appreciates the personal responsibility involved in overcoming affliction; accountability complements the spiritual sensitivity which is so important in both New Age and twelve-step methodologies. The New Age especially appreciates the Third Step: the turning of will and life over to the care of God, however an individual personally understands who or what God is. This allows believers of many faiths to participate in the twelve-step process, a flexibility that characterizes New Age viewpoints and methods. Alcoholics Anonymous was founded independently of other movements and associations commonly considered roots of the New Age. Yet, because of the Twelve Steps' holistic and spiritual nature, many align AA and similar groups with the New Age movement.

Countless Catholics and members of other faiths belong to AA and other groups based on the Twelve Steps. The Church welcomes and encourages the personal recovery these groups foster. The element of recompense, as well as the principles promoted in the other eleven steps, corresponds conspicuously with Christian beliefs and practices. Jesus taught: "When you are offering your gift at the altar, if you remember that your brother or sister has something against you, leave your gift there before the altar and go; first be reconciled to your brother or sister, and then come and offer your gift" (Matthew 5:23-24).

## Is it right to use higher consciousness to make more money or to improve one's business?

Clearly, many New Age elements have moved into the corporate world, influencing approaches to financial success. Induced by factors like meditation, reliance on herbs and crystals, positive thought, forgiveness, and activation of psychic energy, higher consciousness is a dynamic source of creativity and productivity. In business and finance, these kinds of energies can significantly and positively affect profit lines and income. Consequently we find salespersons, managers, and CEOs listening to tapes, attending workshops, and taking counsel from spiritual masters; these activities reflect New Age perspectives and techniques. Participants and their enterprises sometimes interact and support one another through networks and directories, prompting personal development. Often personal transformation leads to professional and commercial achievement. Higher consciousness and prosperity, reflecting a new self-image and divine abundance, can exist comfortably together.

As with any sound and respectable movement, New Age practices can deteriorate into undue individualism, selfishness, and exploitation. Business-oriented New Age philosophies and methodologies, however, typically include a global perspective. Environmental and social concerns often receive emphasis, thus keeping higher consciousness as a component of universal love sharply in focus. Business and professional advancement must be inseparable from the acceptance of ethical responsibilities. The greater good of others, in the workplace and in society, must be considered. Communities, nations, and races should benefit from New Age interests and practices.

The Bible clearly states that God may bless the righteous person with prosperity: "God gives wealth and possessions and…he enables [them] to enjoy…and to accept their lot and find enjoyment in their toil—this is the gift of God" (Ecclesiastes 5:19; see also Deuteronomy 8:18, 1 Samuel 2:7, and Proverbs 10:22). Jesus promised that those who left everything—including family and possessions—to follow him would receive a hundred-fold familial and earthly blessings (Matthew 19:29).

Yet the unrighteous enjoy affluence and the righteous face danger from their riches, forsaking their faith and God from whom prosperity comes. The prosperous must remember that their wealth was not attained solely through their efforts (Deuteronomy 8:17-18) but only with God's help (Psalm 127:1). Enjoyment of money and possessions often leads to an insatiable desire for more (Ecclesiastes 5:10), closes us to God's word (Matthew 13:22), and invites "senseless and harmful desires that plunge people into ruin and destruction" (1 Timothy 6:9). Jesus teaches that "it will be hard for a rich person to enter the kingdom of heaven" (Matthew 19:23). Prosperity itself is not evil, but it potentially distracts us from authentic faith. Paul advocates a proper use of wealth that balances need and abundance (2 Corinthians 8:13-14). John asks, "How does God's love abide in anyone who has the world's goods and sees a brother or sister in need and yet refuses help?" (1 John 3:17). Timothy cautions Christians to avoid excess accumulation (1 Timothy 6:17).

These directives, however, lack a precision that avoids all ambiguities. We accumulate and use wealth for different reasons; we adopt different perspectives about our responsibilities. Some of us have too much and others give more than is really helpful. While recognizing the benefits of profits, the *Catechism of the Catholic Church* teaches that business leaders must "consider the good of persons" while being "responsible to society for the economic and ecological effects" of business operations (2432). Pope John Paul II repeatedly challenges us to find a just and loving middle ground between excessive capitalism (where individuals and groups have too much) and excessive socialism (where individuals and groups are given too much). Working toward this middle ground will help us fulfill the mandate of the Second Vatican Council: "Every effort must be made to put an end as soon as possible to the immense economic inequalities which exist in the world and increase from day to day" (*Pastoral Constitution on the Church in the Modern World*, 66). Wealth can be a blessing, but it must be enjoyed carefully.

### How realistic is the New Age dream of world peace?

Concerns for earth's ecological well-being and a global sense of the basic spiritual solidarity of all reality lead many in the New Age movement to long for and expect universal harmony. No longer devastated by pollution and other environmental abuses, the earth would be whole and healed. No longer threatened, maimed, and massacred by conventional, biological, and nuclear weapons, humanity could rest secure in a worldwide experience of concord and love. New Age environmental, social, and pacifist interests have taken the form of practical political strategies in the West, especially in Europe. Throughout the world, however, New Age enthusiasts demonstrate solidarity through their acceptance of visualization as a powerful tool of peace. Individually and through organizations, they commit themselves to thinking of and imaging peace in personal and international relations. Beginning with desired improvements close to home and trusting in the power of mind over matter, the New Age movement is thus thought to be able to effect planetary transformation.

Universal peace is a major biblical theme. *Shalom*, the Hebrew greeting of peace, conveys a wish and prayer for wholeness and tranquillity. These divine blessings will come to those who turn to God and remain faithful. "Steadfast love and faithfulness will meet; / righteousness and peace will kiss each other" (Psalm 85:10). This expectancy reverberates throughout the Old Testament prophecies of wonderful things to come: a new time and age when ruin, mourning, and darkness give way to new joy in the light of God (Isaiah 60:17-22). The coming of the Messiah inaugurated such an age. Christians, therefore, base their hopes for peace on Jesus who through his example and teaching guides them "into the way of peace" (Luke 1:79). He gives his own peace to others (John 14:27). By his cross and resurrection he has brought peace, reconciling the world to God (Colossians 1:20). Surely today's sorrows and wars, however, give ample evidence that spiritual renewal has not reached everyone and everything. Therefore, Christians must still strive lovingly for peace, believing they are saved and trusting in God's promise of "new heavens and a new earth" (2 Peter 3:11-15).

We must accept with lively faith God's gift of peace to the world. We must also accept its challenge to act according to divine designs. Catholic teachings have repeatedly called sons and daughters of the church and all persons of good will to the task of peacemaking. Humanity "is everywhere more conscious of its own unity," Vatican II proclaimed, yet the true humanization of the world requires that all devote themselves "to the cause of true peace with renewed vigor." For this, a loving respect for all persons' dignity is essential. We must take crucial steps to prevent needless and immoral brutalities: we must learn to recognize the horrors of modern warfare, to determine the difference between a just war of defense and one aimed at imposing domination, and to realistically assess the danger of an arms race. Vatican II urged world leaders to foster "mutual trust between peoples…[and to] enlarge their thoughts and their spirit beyond the confines of their own country," becoming more conscious of a humanity "which is painstakingly advancing towards greater maturity." These leaders need support in their task to form in persons' minds "renewed sentiments of peace." This "change of heart" can lead us to anticipate realistically an enduring peace (*Pastoral Constitution on the Church in the Modern World*, 77-82).

# SEVEN

# New Age and Catholic?

***Can a Catholic participate in the New Age movement?***

The characteristics of persons associated with the New Age movement include:

- striving to attain an ever-higher consciousness of the spiritual realm and the responsibilities that go with this awareness
- in an ecumenical spirit, respecting the sincere and reputable beliefs of other persons and peoples
- in a spirit of sharing and solidarity, appropriately adapting these beliefs to their one's personal creeds and spiritual practices
- praying and meditating, sometimes using visualization and guided imagery
- relaxing through enjoyment of calming music
- believing that all reality is unified or one because of divine power and presence
- trusting the influence of mind over matter and psychic powers
- showing concern for the environment
- using natural products like herbs and minerals to facilitate health and awareness
- viewing health and healing as parts of a holistic process, hoping for an improved physical existence in a future life;
- appreciating an ability to enjoy contact with the dead for beneficial purposes
- respecting the value of dreams

- aspiring to universal love and forgiveness
- responsibly enjoying material goods
- working for world peace

These traits, though typical, are not manifested by every proponent of New Age philosophy and techniques. And the intensity of each trait varies among individuals.

From the New Age perspective, Catholics who manifest some, most, or all of these New Age traits can be considered participants in the New Age movement, even if the Catholics themselves are unaware of the movement or its manifestation in them. Discriminating observers, however, note the differences that distinguish Catholics from others generally associated with the New Age. The life and spirituality of Catholics revolves around faith in Jesus Christ and his Church. Ecumenism must not compromise this faith. Catholic theology regarding creation and grace excludes a pantheistic view of reality. Catholics reverence sacramentals (salt, water, and oil, for example) because these elements have been blessed, not merely because they possess inherent powers. Catholics clearly accept the biblical teaching that illness and suffering are not necessarily punishments for immoral or unhealthy choices. Catholic teachings depict resurrection of the body after death but not multiple recurrences of bodily existence. Nevertheless, an extraordinary degree of unanimity exists between Catholic and New Age beliefs and practices. Catholics, therefore, may support and adopt any New Age supposition, perspective, and practice not at odds with Catholic teachings.

### Can someone in the New Age movement become a Catholic without giving up anything?

Despite the unanimity between Catholicism and the New Age, significant distinguishing factors exist. New Age enthusiasts who feel called to follow Jesus Christ and accept a new life of faith, who are attracted to centuries-old communal traditions and customs, who respond to the renewing spirit of the Second Vatican Council, and who willingly give appropriate recognition to biblical and ecclesiastical authority will probably have difficulty adhering to all former beliefs and practices. Yet catholicity and universality have marked the Roman Church precisely because the Church has historically recognized the value of diversity within its boundaries. From this perspective, participants in the New Age movement find welcome in Catholicism; they can expect that any changes will be more those of adaptation than loss.

# Related Readings

Bolen, Jean Shinoda. *The Tao of Psychology: Synchronicity.* San Francisco: Harper, 1982. (A psychiatrist's explanation of how the paranormal works.)

Boyd, Doug. *Mystics, Magicians, and Medicine People: Tales of a Wanderer.* New York: Paragon House, 1989. (A quite readable exploration of folk practices which interest proponents of the New Age.)

Capra, Fritjof. *The Tao of Physics: An Exploration of the Parallels Between Modern Physics and Eastern Mysticism.* New York: Shambhala Publications, 1991. (A clear, though at times challenging, summary of issues which link New Age insight and modern science.)

Carey, Ken. *Return of the Bird Tribes.* San Francisco: Harper, 1991. (A pleasant depiction of higher consciousness and its relationship to the divine.)

Christeann, Aaron, J.P. Hall and M.C. Clark. *Michael: The Basic Teachings.* Orinda, CA: Progress, 1988. (An introductory presentation of channeling and reincarnation psychology.)

Clancy, John et al. *A New Age Guide: For the Thoroughly Confused and Absolutely Certain.* Eastsound, WA: Sweet Forever Publications, 1988. (An easy-to-read summary of New Age interests. Contains valuable annotated bibliographies.)

Ferguson, Marilyn. *The Aquarian Conspiracy: Personal and Social Transformation in the 1980s.* Los Angeles: Tarcher, 1981. (A long but readable account of most aspects of the emerging New Age movement. Has become something of a classic.)

Granberg-Michaelson, Wesley, ed. *Tending the Garden: Essays on the Gospel and the Earth.* Grand Rapids, MI: Eerdmans, 1987. (Essays by Christian scholars on ecological interests related to those of the New Age movement.)

Haring, Herman, and Johann-Baptist Metz, eds. *Reincarnation or Resurrection?* Maryknoll, NY: Orbis, 1993. (Prominent scholars' thoughtful essays on reincarnation and how belief in it relates to Christian teachings and practices.)

Heaney, John J. *The Sacred and the Psychic: Parapsychology and Christian Theology.* New York: Paulist, 1984. (A theologian's clear investigation into the paranormal in the Catholic tradition. A valuable resource for *Catholic Answers to Questions about the New Age Movement.*)

Judy, Dwight H. *Christian Meditation and Inner Healing.* New York: Crossroad, 1991. (A fine alignment of spirituality with holistic interests important to the New Age movement.)

Karpinski, Gloria D. *Where Two Worlds Touch: Spiritual Rites of Passage.* New York: Ballantine, 1990. (Practical application of New Age principles from a psychological point of view.)

Kelly, Mary Olsen, ed. *The Fireside Treasury of Light Anthologies.* New York: Simon and Schuster, 1990. (A collection of excerpts from a variety of New Age writings.)

Keyes, Ken, Jr., *Handbook to Higher Consciousness.* Coos Bay, OR: Love Line Books, 1975. (Very popular classical guide to greater happiness through healthier thinking.)

Maloney, George. *Mysticism and the New Age: Christic Consciousness in the New Creation.* New York: Alba House, 1990. (The prominent Jesuit spiritual writer's sensitive and mostly positive evaluation of the New Age movement.)

Melton, J. Gordon et al. *New Age Almanac.* New York: Visible Ink, 1991. (Detailed treatment of nearly every known aspect and personality of the New Age movement. More information than one can possibly utilize in a single lifetime. A valuable resource for *Catholic Answers to Questions about the New Age Movement.*)

Miller, Ron, and Jim Kenney, eds. *Fireball and the Lotus: Emerging Spirituality from Ancient Roots.* Santa Fe, NM: Bear, 1987. (Essays by Jewish and Christian scholars on the implications of many New Age themes for modern religiousness.)

"New Age Spirituality," *The Way* 33, no. 3 (July 1993). A journal of contemporary spirituality. (A fine collection of articles, mostly by Catholics, on the history and current relevance of the New Age movement.)

Quillo, Ronald. *Companions in Consciousness: The Bible and the New Age Movement.* Liguori, MO: Triumph, 1994. (A probing comparison of biblical faith and New Age awareness.)

Siegel, Bernie S. *Peace, Love and Healing: Bodymind Communication and the Path to Self-Healing: An Exploration.* San Francisco: Harper, 1990. (A prominent physician's guide to holistic health.)

Steindl-Rast, David. *A Listening Heart: The Art of Contemplative Living.* New York: Crossroad, 1983. (A Catholic monk's association of New Age themes with Christian spirituality.)

Streiker, Lowell D. *New Age Comes to Main Street: What Worried Christians Must Know.* Nashville: Abingdon, 1990. (A Christian's calm assessment of the value of the New Age movement.)

Zukav, Gary. *The Seat of the Soul.* New York: Simon & Schuster, 1990. (A brief and orderly exploration of several New Age themes.)

## Also by Ronald Quillo

### Companions in Consciousness
### The Bible and the New Age Movement
This incisive work is written for anyone who wonders how/if the beliefs and practices of the current New Age movement compare with the teachings of the Bible. $18.95

## More Titles on Religious Topics

### The Ground We Share
### Everyday Practice, Buddhist and Christian
#### by Robert Aitken and David Steindl-Rast
A Buddhist and a Christian—both distinguished religious thinkers—meet here in private retreat to discuss the fundamental nature of the religious experience and the problems of leading a deeply spiritual and upright life in the modern world. $17.95

### Reinhabiting the Earth
### Biblical Perspectives and Eco-Spiritual Reflections
#### by Mary Lou Van Rossum
Amid global and human crises of historic proportions, there is a need for understanding and revering our world—and above all, for recognizing our responsibility for bringing about a new creation, a new order of being. This unique book gives a biblical perspective to our role in the face of ecological choices and human survival. $18.95